What's in Style decks

CRE TIVE
HOMEOWNER®

What's in Style decks

Lynn Elliott

CREATIVE HOMEOWNER®, Upper Saddle River, New Jersey

Editorial Director: Timothy O. Bakke
Creative Director: Clarke Barre
Art Director: Monduane Harris
Production Manager: Kimberly H. Vivas

Senior Editor, Decorating Books: Kathie Robitz
Associate Editor: Linda Stonehill
Copy Editor: Ellie Sweeney
Proofreader: Laura De Ferrari
Photo Research: Lynn Elliott, Amla Sanghvi, Stanley Sudol
Indexer: Joanne M. Still

Book Designer: Monduane Harris
Illustrations: Ian Warpole
Cover Design: Monduane Harris
Front Cover Photography: Mark Lohman
Back Cover Photography: *(top, all except far right)* John Kelly;
(far right) Summit;
(bottom) Michael Thompson

Manufactured in the United States of America
Current Printing (last digit)
10 9 8 7 6 5 4 3 2 1

What's in Style — Decks, First Edition
Library of Congress Catalog Card Number: 00-107265
ISBN: 1-58011-092-4

CREATIVE HOMEOWNER PRESS®
A Division of Federal Marketing Corp.
24 Park Way, Upper Saddle River, NJ 07458
Web site: **www.creativehomeowner.com**

Acknowledgments

"Too many cooks may spoil the broth," but that is not the case with books. It took many helping hands — and words of advice — to create this book. I would like to thank everyone who offered their assistance, especially The California Redwood Association, The Southern Pine Council, deck builder Ray Walsh, and Zan-ell Construction.

Special thanks goes to my editor, Kathie Robitz, for her calm guidance, quick humor, and infinite patience.

Contents

Introduction

A **deck** is **uniquely** equipped
to **blend** the elements of **nature**
with the **comforts** of home. In fact, . . .

a great deck can be a fabulous getaway—right in your own backyard. It's a place to indulge in relaxing pleasures—reading, sunbathing, a soak in a hot tub, or gathering with family and friends—while enjoying the outdoors. If you're building a new deck, one of the first things you'll have to consider is the site. Few are perfect. Perhaps the lot slopes or is too narrow, or maybe your neighbor's house is too close by, creating a privacy issue. If you have an existing deck, it may lack style, or perhaps it's too small for your needs. *What's In Style—Decks* offers numerous ideas and a portfolio of pictures with livable solutions to common deck challenges. If you're looking for inspiration, it's all here.

beforehand—how often you entertain and which activities you may want to enjoy on your deck. Then it discusses the practical matter of the site—the size and the landscape. A deck on a small lot may require careful planning; one on a large lot may need to be broken up into smaller, perhaps multilevel, zones.

Chapter 2, "Design," gives you a chance to a view an array of ground-level, raised, or multilevel decks. Ground-level decks are great for small yards, raised decks work for sloped lots, and multilevel designs are the best option for expansive spaces. You'll find great examples of each type in this section.

Just beyond these elegant french doors are two front-row seats to the great outdoors.

Chapter 1, "Planning," addresses all of the issues you'll need to examine

Looking for a way to add character to your deck? Go to Chapter 3, "Details." If you think all decks look alike, you're in for a surprise. Handsome architectural features — such as railings, decking patterns, built-ins, and stairs — take your deck from the ordinary to unique. Plus, if you're trying to find a way to blend the deck with the style of your house, details provide the answer.

Chapter 4, "Lighting," offers information about this often-ignored aspect of design. Most homeowners will want to use a deck day and night. This means that they'll need lighting for dining, cooking, and conversation areas. Safety is another good reason to consider lighting. Plus, in this high-tech age, access to electricity and phone lines is important, even outdoors where you may want to work on your portable laptop computer. This chapter reviews all of the possibilities.

Deck Lifestyle

What's In Style—Decks also covers the lifestyle issues regarding your deck — furnishings, cooking essentials, shade coverings, and water features. These are the elements that make the space truly inviting. Many of these accessories also make your deck function more smoothly while enhancing your enjoyment.

Chapter 5, "Furniture," addresses what may be the most important amenity you can add to your deck. For your comfort, as well as for the sake of your budget, review all of the options including wood, metal, resin, and reed furniture. Get the lowdown on what you'll need and how much care is involved with each type.

Next to furniture, cooking and its related equipment are essential ingredients in the success and enjoyment of a deck. Grilling is, after all, one of America's favorite pastimes. To make sure you pick the right grill, Chapter 6, "Cooking and Entertaining," weighs the options. Outdoor kitchens are becoming more popular because of their convenience. Learn what countertop materials are best and where to locate a fresh-air kitchen. This chapter also provides an overview on portable bars and refrigerators that can withstand the elements.

Decks and the Environment

As much as we may seek out the sun, there are times when less of it is welcome. Chapter 7, "Shade," reviews the alternatives for coverings. You may prefer something permanent, such as a roof, pergola, or gazebo, but removable options, including awnings, shade cloths, and sun tents are decorative, too. Each type has its own means of improving the look and function of your deck.

Chapter 8, "Adding Water," makes a splash as it covers pools, spas, and water features that can be incorporated into your deck plan. When combined with a deck, a pool or spa becomes a major outdoor attraction. Water features can be as simple as a reflecting basin or as complex as a man-made pond.

With time, you can turn ideas for your outdoor space into a beautiful deck. The following pages are meant to stimulate your creative thinking so that you can design the deck of your dreams. A well-planned design is a reflection of your style — an extension of yourself as well as of your home. By doing some advanced planning now, you'll be able to sit back with a cold drink and relax later.

A small and sunny raised deck is a natural extension to this home's covered porch.

Planning

If you've been thinking about building a deck,

you probably want extra living space

for you and your family...

but you may also need more. Ever consider a place for casual entertaining? How about including a fully appointed outdoor kitchen in your deck plans? Or maybe the deck of your dreams is a quiet getaway, a spot for relaxing in a hot tub or napping in a hammock. Whatever the case, a well-designed deck always makes a pleasing transition from house to garden.

If you plan the deck with the same consideration you give to the rooms inside your home, it will reflect your lifestyle needs while adding value to your property. Your budget and the site will be

primary factors in determining the kind of deck you build. But the existing landscape, your home's architectural style, and what kind of living space you're hoping to gain will influence you as well. Look around your neighborhood for ideas. Take snapshots of your favorite designs. Talk to architects and contractors or the professionals at home centers. Keep a notebook or a folder of your thoughts, photos from magazines, and any advice you receive. Don't forget to include the important phone numbers of the professionals with whom you have consulted as well as any references and their comments.

When you plan any living space, always factor traffic patterns into the layout. Think about the pathways from

This step-down design compensates for a sloped lot. It also provides dining, conversation, and viewing areas.

Design Quiz

Your notes might also include a list of questions that only you can answer. Some of these might be:

▶ What are your family's activities and habits? Do they like sunbathing, swimming, or outdoor cooking and dining?

▶ Do you like to entertain? How large of a group?

▶ Do you prefer a formal or informal look? A formal deck may include a gazebo or other classical elements; an informal deck may incorporate a hot tub and built-in benches into the plan.

▶ Do you require an outdoor kitchen complete with appliances, or is a small spot for the grill adequate for your needs?

▶ Will young children play on the deck? Will a guest or family member need special access, such as a ramp?

▶ Do you prefer sun or shade? Will you require partial or complete shading? A privacy wall?

▶ How much time are you willing to devote to maintenance?

your house to the grill and between conversation areas and dining areas. For safety, make sure there will be clear access near stairs, ramps, or doors.

The Site

How large is the site? Is the ground level or sloped? Which side of the house receives the most sun? Is your yard near the street? How much privacy do you want? All of these questions influence where you will locate your deck and how large it will be. A small site doesn't have to limit your plans for living large outdoors, however.

Look at the direction of the sun to see whether the deck receives strong light all day (a southern exposure), in the morning (an eastern exposure), late in the afternoon (a western exposure), or not at all (a northern exposure). What about wind? Vertical elements or fences can buffer these forces.

This custom-designed deck allows the homeowners to retain an existing tree that acts as a privacy screen.

1. A deck doesn't have to be large to be enjoyed. This second-story deck is an ample open-air getaway. **2.** This multilevel deck makes an attractive transition from yard to house. **3.** Even a basic rectangle can be divided into separate zones. **4.** When planning the deck's dining area, be sure you have a way to get food safely from the grill to the table, and allow enough room to get in and out of chairs easily.

Sunlight . . . is an important factor in locating your deck. Excessive exposure without shading can be too hot. Choose a spot that receives some natural shade, or plan on a covering to keep everyone comfortable.

Privacy . . . is often a desirable element. Use plantings, such as trees and shrubs, for a natural shield. The other option is a privacy screen: high fences in addition to plantings can buffer street noises as well as nosy neighbors.

Views . . . of the natural surroundings of your site add to its appeal. Position the deck so that you can see the vista unobstructed. If you don't have a view, create one. It could be the focal point of your garden, a fountain, or even a handsome tree. ✪

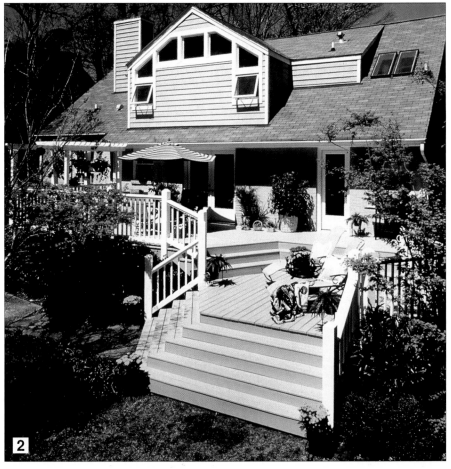

3

4

1. Some sites are more challenging than others but worth the special structural considerations. This deck overlooks the coastline and offers a dramatic view of the ocean. **2.** A raised deck overcomes most site problems. Here, a combination of uncovered and covered areas permits deck use even on rainy days. **3.** Open-riser wooden stairs framed by trees and hedges blend into the surroundings and make a pleasing transition to a garden area.

1. An expansive multilevel deck is an excellent way to landscape a large site.
2. Framing the sides of these shallow steps with flowers helps to safely define the edges without the use of a railing.
3. When siting a deck, always take advantage of a great view (such as a lake), and check the location's exposure to sunlight and wind. 4. Instead of entirely enclosing a deck with a fence, install a trellis or a planter to screen it from onlookers or street noise.
5. A ramp is a practical way to make a deck accessible to everyone. Check building codes to make sure the ramp conforms to local regulations.

DESIGN TIP

Consider using a computer-aided design (CAD) program to plan your deck. Some programs let you see three-dimensional views of your design complete with railings, stairs, planters, hot tubs, and the surrounding landscaping.

1. Make aesthetic elements part of the plan. This pergola features widely spaced rafters to create pleasing shadows on the woodwork as the sun filters through it. 2. If a pool is part of your landscape, be sure to include it in the siting plans for your deck. 3. This versatile deck has an outdoor table and sitting area for warm weather and an enclosed area for cool and rainy days. 4. The built-in benches along the sides of this deck provide threefold benefits: as seating, as a railing, and as a partial privacy wall.

3

4

Design

When designing a deck, consider
the various types: attached or freestanding,
ground level or raised, single level or multilevel, . . .

and explore the advantages and disadvantages of each. Some determining factors are simply practical. An attached deck offers direct access to the house as well as to the utilities. It also creates a logical transition between the house and the garden. However, a freestanding deck lets you choose the best location with regard to site conditions, sun and wind exposure, privacy, and view. A ground-level deck is the simplest type to build and is typically less expensive than a raised or multi-tiered design because it doesn't require stairs and railings. But if you want a deck design that has more pizzazz than a plain four-sided shape has to offer, consider a curved, hexagonal, or even octagonal design.

A deck on a sloped lot is divided into conversation, dining, and viewing areas. The smooth transition between each of these zones makes the space excellent for entertaining, too.

Your choice will also depend on the landscape and architectural design of your home as well as on

general aesthetics. A good design incorporates proper *scale* and *proportion:* the size and shape of the deck should complement the house. To exceed the ordinary, incorporate different *lines* into your design: vertical, horizontal, diagonal, and curved. You can do this not only with the shape of the deck but also with other design elements. The flooring pattern, plants and planters, and furnishings offer numerous opportunities to vary the lines and shapes in the deck's design and decoration.

When considering all of these things, remember the importance of *balance* and *harmony.* If the stairs are prominent and located on one side of the deck, create balance with another architectural or decorative feature of similar weight on the other side. Pull the look together with a harmonious blend of styles, colors, and patterns. Let repeated shapes and motifs around the deck create movement or *rhythm* that leads the eye from the entrance onto the deck to the various zones of cooking, dining, the hot tub, the garden, and so forth.

Materials and Finishes

Traditionally, decks have been constructed of wood—typically redwood, western red cedar, or pressure-treated southern pine, and lately Alaska yellow cedar and tropical hardwoods. Thanks to technology, there are two new categories of decking: *composite,* which is made of natural fiber and recycled plastic, and *extruded vinyl.*

You can paint or stain wood or allow it to weather naturally, but most wood decks need some protection from the elements. Occasional treatment with a wood preservative will help prevent decay. Wood decks also require a water-repellent finish to keep the wood from shrinking

or splintering. Periodic maintenance with mildew remover is important, too.

Stains are oil- or water-based. Semitransparent stains reveal the wood's grain; opaque stains can hide wood flaws. Like stains, paints for decks are oil- or water-based. Paint conceals the grain of the wood as well as its flaws. No matter which you use—paint or stain—each can wear over time, and climate plays a role in their ability to hold up against the elements.

Composite decking is an easy-care material. Some types require no stain or sealants, and you can clean them with detergents found in home centers. Vinyl decking won't rot or warp, and maintenance is also easy. It needs no finish. To keep this decking clean, just hose it down with water periodically.

1. Stained or left natural, wood blends well into the surrounding landscape. Pillows add domestic accents to the wild outdoors. **2.** Regular maintenance and a water-repellent stain finish fight off the effects of salty sea air.

2

1. A bench near the stairs is a handy place to drop off a towel or toys. Never clutter stairs. **2.** A multi-tiered deck is accessible from different levels of a house. **3.** Besides providing shade, this tree steals attention away from the distant mountain view.

DESIGN TIP

Arrange outdoor spaces as you would an interior room. Choose a dominant element around which everything else flows. It can be a pool, a fire pit, or the garden. One major furniture piece, such as a dining table, can anchor an area.

1. Simple grouped furniture and pretty potted flowers create a charming outdoor sitting room. **2.** Make your deck as lush as your garden by surrounding it with plants, such as the wisteria cascading onto this deck from the overhang above. **3.** Adding color with handsome painted furniture, for example, is an easy way to spice up a simple design plan.

4

1. Make a deck cozy with vintage-style furniture and details like this faux carpet created with paint and stain. 2. A sleek dining table and chairs take nothing away from the view from this contemporary deck design. 3. Simple seating blends with the cedar shakes and stained decking of this New England home. 4. The color of this stain complements this Southern California house's trim and clay-tile roof. 5. Wooden decking can also be used as a walkway or path leading to a gazebo in a secluded part of the yard.

Ground-level decks . . . resemble a low platform and are best for flat locations. They can be the most economical type to build because they don't require stairs.

Raised decks . . . can rise just a few steps up or meet the second story of a house. Lifted high on post supports, they adapt well to uneven or sloped locations.

Multilevel decks . . . feature two or more stories and are connected by stairways or ramps. They can follow the contours of a sloped lot, unifying the deck with the outdoors. ✸

5

1. Herringbone brick pavers lead toward this deck. 2. This siding and pergola work harmoniously with these decking materials. 3. Wicker and white pickets look charming in this deck setting.

DESIGN TIP

A single-level deck can use a strong vertical element, such as a pergola or a gazebo, to make it interesting. A simple and less-expensive option is a potted conical shrub or a clematis growing on a trellis.

Details

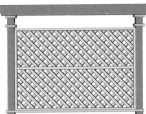

Railing styles and decking patterns

offer opportunities to bring individuality

and unique details to your deck's design . . .

and built-in benches and planters break up space creatively. In the case of planters, you can also add color to your deck with plants and flowers. Stairs can be more than functional, too. Depending on their width and length, they create visual impact on your deck. A privacy fence can be a part of the deck or the landscape, and it should complement your decorative scheme. This chapter will show you a portfolio of design ideas that make the most of these types of details. Take the time to review them so that you choose something that reflects your personal style and ties in with your deck's architectural design.

A built-in bench and planters add character to a wide staircase here. A lattice wall provides privacy and light screening from the sun.

Railings

Most railings are made from wood, clear acrylic, tempered glass, metal, or wire cable. But whatever the material, the design of the railing has to be strong enough to support the weight of an adult who is leaning against or sitting on it. There are four styles to choose from: post and rail, picket, panel, and post and cable, which is a variation on the post and rail style.

DESIGN TIP

Install caps and post finials to your railings. A rail cap protects the cut ends of the posts from the weather. Finials add another decorative layer to your design, and the styles are endless—ball, chamfered, grooved, and top hat are a few.

A *post-and-rail style* has a number of parts: support posts, rails, balusters, and, usually, a railing cap. Support posts are attached to the end joists and headers of the deck so that they are an integral part of the structure. Horizontal rails run between the vertical posts, creating the basic, one-dimensional frame for the railing. Balusters, or decorative posts, give railings character. They create the vertical patterns in between the support posts. Balusters can be simple 2x2s, turned spindles, or plain one-by lumber. A *railing cap* is an optional horizontal piece that fits over the top of the railing.

A *picket* is a vertical board with a decorative top—that may be curved, pointed, or notched. Pickets stand side by side along a basic railing. Pickets are not as popular for railings as they are for fences because they will block most of a view. There are situations where you may prefer the privacy they offer, however.

An Alternative

Post-and-cable railings consist of metal posts and wire cables that are attached to the posts by a hook-and-eye system. This type of railing complements contemporary-style decks and doesn't obscure a view.

Panels are occasionally preferable to decorative posts and are made of wood, clear acrylic, or tempered glass. Acrylic and glass panels are favored for decks with spectacular vistas because virtually nothing blocks a view of the scenery. But keep maintenance in mind because these panels will need regular cleaning. For example, if you live by the ocean, sea spray can build up on the panels, and you will have to hose them down and wipe them dry on a regular basis.

Check your local codes for specifications on the distance between posts, the openings below railings, and the spacing of balusters. In general, railings should be 36 to 42 inches high. Support posts are usually spaced 4 feet apart. Most local codes specify spacing balusters 4 inches or less apart to prevent children from squeezing through and falling off the deck. If your deck is less than 18 inches aboveground, a railing isn't required, but you should consider one for safety. Where railings are required, local building codes may not allow horizontal designs (with no balusters). Check with the local building inspector.

Decking Patterns

You may never have considered the layout of the floorboards of a deck, but you have more options than just placing the boards perpendicularly to the joists. Pattern choices include diagonal, basket weave, framed, geometric grid, or herringbone. Each one of these styles can have a different visual effect on your deck. Some patterns make a deck appear larger; others will contract space visually. Assess design choices based on the size of your deck.

Diagonal decking seemingly enlarges the look of a small deck because the angled lines of the boards draw the eye across the deck. A basket-weave pattern (small squares made with five or six boards set perpendicularly to each other in an alternating pattern) can have the opposite effect, making a large deck cozier because the squares break up the space visually. *Framed decking* encloses the space. It has a border with mitered corners set around a

Railings can add style. A few examples: **1.** Mediterranean style; **2.** traditional; **3.** rounded cottage-style picket; **4.** hook-and-eye wire cable; **5.** contemporary metal; **6.** cast iron.

Decking patterns add style underfoot. **1.** Herringbone decking meets in a V-shaped pattern. **2.** Radial decking sets this arbor apart. **3.** This complex decking pattern is costly but impressive. **4.** A checkered decking pattern adds symmetry to this space. **5.** The railing treatment on the same deck reinforces the orderliness that pattern can effect.

Simplify . . . your design. For instance, if your railing is an elaborate Chinese-Chippendale style, you may want to keep the design of benches, planters, and decking basic to prevent visual competition between the elements. ✿

4

center of straight or diagonal boards. Framed decking creates well-defined areas or zones. Use it if you want one area of the deck to appear distinct from the overall space. *Geometric decking* is similar to the basketweave pattern, except that the small squares are set diagonally to each other, visually expanding the space. *Herringbone decking* consists of alternating boards in a V-shaped layout.

Remember that these complex designs require more wood because of increased waste. This makes the designs more expensive and time-intensive to install.

5

The seat back should also be tilted 5 to 10 degrees for comfort. The depth of the seat is usually 18 inches, and it should be about 15 to 18 inches from the floor. Add hinges to the seat of a bench to create extra storage.

A *cantilevered bench* is another type of built-in. The back can be part of a planter. Basically, a cantilevered bench is made of a single large planter with a seat that extends from one or more of its sides. This type of bench is used to create permanent separations between different areas on the deck.

A *backless built-in bench* is a low and unobtrusive way to provide built-in seating. Without a back, it won't substitute for a railing. But the bench is an easy addition to a ground-level deck, and it can make a practical

Plus you'll have to decide on a pattern and plan the framing layout carefully in advance so that all of the members are supported properly.

Built-ins

Built-ins are some of the most useful extras you can add to your deck. When worked into the overall design, built-ins add seating and storage, control traffic, divide space, and add visual interest. Built-in benches often replace sections of the railing and are made of the same material as the deck for a unified look. You can choose between benches with or without a back. The backrest of built-in seating is similar to a railing, so it must be sturdy. Because children may stand on a bench, it should be higher than the railing—typically 15 to 18 inches higher.

3

1. Built-in planters work well with broad, gently rising stairs, especially at turns or near landings. 2. Planters built on gravel allow excess water to drain into the soil. 3. The open-slat design on these benches lets water fall through, preventing puddles from forming on the seats. 4. Benches define the edge of this overhang while providing extra seating.

4

1. A pot of colorful flowers is a pretty detail you can place anywhere. **2.** Throw a couple of pillows on a built-in bench and voilà—a reading nook. **3.** Vary container heights for more interest. **4.** Make sure planters attached to railings are securely bolted to prevent mishaps. **5.** Curved balusters add a handsome custom-designed touch to these railings. **6.** A tiered staircase is an attractive feature, but wide stairs require extra stringers for support.

border at level changes on a large deck. Aside from basic benches, there are potting benches, which are built between two planters. It is typical for the bench seat to consist of slats spaced up to about 2 inches apart for drainage.

Built-in planters add another layer to your design—one that helps introduce color and beauty to the deck with flowering plants. Planters can be incorporated into most decks. You'll find them next to benches, as a part of the stairs, or as a divider between deck levels. The sizes and heights of planters vary, but there are a few guidelines.

Planters on potting benches generally stand between 23 to 26 inches high and 21 to 24 inches wide. Freestanding planters can range from 8 to 10 inches deep for plants and 18 to 24 inches deep for shrubs. It's practical to raise planters off the deck floor to allow air to circulate underneath. In addition, planters on wheels or casters let you rearrange the space on your deck at will.

Stairs

Besides their functional role, stairs play an aesthetic part in your deck's architectural design. On the practical side, there may be specific building codes about the rise and run of your stairs, so become familiar with them. (The

Place . . . your details with care. Use benches and planters to control the flow of movement across your deck, not interrupt it. Avoid contrived placement. For instance, don't run a series of benches down the center of a deck just to create two separate areas. Instead, try a cantilevered bench that projects out from a railing or wall instead of floating in the middle of the deck. The combination of seat and planter makes this divider more substantial and effective. ✺

rise is the height of the deck; the unit rise is the height of the step; the run is the length of the stairway; the unit run is the depth of the step.) The most comfortable unit rise is 4 to 7 inches. If your deck's rise will measure more than 8 feet, consider breaking up the staircase with a landing.

Aesthetically, stairs draw the eyes upward and, particularly in the case of multi-tiered stairways, make the transition from the garden to the deck a gentle one. Depending on the architectural and decorative details you add, stairs help to define the style of the structure as well.

Fences

If the neighboring houses are too close to your deck, a privacy fence can help. It can also buffer the deck against harsh weather. Most privacy fences are at least 6

1. Vines soften the look of this privacy fence. The narrow slats allow air and light to filter onto the deck. **2.** Near the water and salty air, a railing cap and decorative post tops protect the open grain at the top of the balusters and the structural posts from weather damage.

feet high. Again, check with your local building department for code regulations
to see whether you need a variance for a fence this high.

If you want to block the wind but not the light, try a louvered or basket-weave
style. Louvered fences allow air to flow onto the deck but interrupt its force.
Basket-weave designs have thin horizontal boards that are "woven" over vertical
posts. They completely block views and wind. Lattice fences let breezes and light
through and enclose a space without confining it. Solid-board fences provide the
most privacy while blocking wind and light. Add a prefabricated lattice top to the
top of the fence to make it less imposing.

DESIGN TIP

An easy way to blend
the new deck with the
architecture of a house
is with railings. Precut
railings and caps come
in many styles and sizes.

Lighting

In terms of lighting and electricity,

a deck can be as fully functional

as any room . . .

inside your house. In addition to natural light, a pleasing combination of even, diffused general (also called "ambient") light, as well as accent and task lighting from artificial sources, can illuminate your deck for use after the sun goes down. Safety and security are two additional considerations that call for lighting, especially at stairways and along paths. At the same time, you can install dimmer switches for the lights, electrical outlets for a blender or a television, and switches for retractable awnings. If you own a notebook computer, you might also want to install telephone jacks so that you can read e-mail, get access to your favorite Web sites, or work on a report while enjoying the fresh air.

Planning

First decide how much light you need and where it should go. Besides general overall illumination, locate fixtures near activity zones: the food preparation and cooking area, the wet bar, or wherever you plan to set up drinks, snacks, or a buffet when you entertain. Be sure that there is adequate light near the dining table, conversation areas, and recreational spots, such as the hot tub, if you plan to use them in the evening. You may want separate switches for each one, and you might consider dimmers; you don't

A simple string of low-tech party lights may be all you need to brighten your deck.

need or want the same intensity of light required for barbecuing as you do for relaxing in the hot tub.

What type of fixtures should you choose? That partly depends on the location. Near a wall or under a permanent roof, sconces and ceiling fixtures will provide light while staying out of the way. For uncovered areas, try post or railing lamps.

Lighting the Way

Walkways and staircases need lighting for safety. There are a number of practical options: path lights (if the walkway is ground level), brick lights that can be inserted into your walls near the steps, and railing fixtures that can be tucked under deck railings or steps. Less-functional but more-decorative lighting such as post lamps can provide illumination for high traffic areas; sconces can be effective on stair landings or near doors. Don't forget about areas that may call for motion-sensitive floodlights: entrances into the house, underneath a raised deck, and deep yards are all excellent locations for floodlights. Keep these fixtures on separate switches so that they don't interfere with the atmosphere you want to create while you are using the deck.

Adding Accent Light

Are there any noteworthy plantings or objects in your garden that you can highlight? By using in-ground accent lighting or spotlights, you can create dramatic nighttime effects or a focal point. Artful lighting can enhance the ambience of your deck by drawing attention to the shape of a handsome tree, a garden statue, a fountain or pond, or an outdoor pool.

Choosing the Right Fixture

If your home is formal, traditional fixtures in brass or an antique finish will complement the overall scheme nicely. For a modern setting, choose streamlined fixtures with matte or brushed-metal finishes. Landscape lighting is often utilitarian, but it is intended to blend unobtrusively into the landscape; the light, not the fixture, is noticeable. Path and post lighting, however, can be decorative and comes in a variety of styles and finishes, from highly polished metals to antique and matte looks.

Depending on the lighting system you buy, you may be able to install the fixtures yourself. But working with electricity does pose technical, code, and safety concerns. It's probably best to hire a qualified professional for the installation. For complex projects, you may also want to consult a lighting professional or a landscape architect. Home centers sometimes provide this type of expertise. If you decide to plot a design yourself, remember not to overlight the deck.

Other Considerations

As you plan to install deck lighting, think about the space's other electrical or wiring needs. If there is an outdoor kitchen, a grill area, or a bar, you may want outlets for a refrigerator or small appliances. You might include additional outlets for a stereo or speakers, or even a TV. Don't overlook a phone jack for your laptop computer. Some decking systems come prewired and are ready to be hooked up. So with forethought, you can incorporate everything you need into your outdoor living plans.

A wall sconce next to the door says "Welcome" and may be all that's needed to illuminate a small area.

1. You can diffuse harsh lighting by placing the fixtures on the outside of the railing. **2.** For safety, railing lights illuminate each turn in this staircase. **3.** Use the same type of fixture in a number of locations to create a unified look. **4.** The beam from a floodlight is too strong for general illumination, but it provides excellent security near entrances. **5.** A combination of fixtures can draw attention to different areas at night.

4

DESIGN TIP

For lighting in hard-to-reach areas, use a lamp (bulb) with a long life so that you don't have to replace it often.

5

General lighting . . . also known as ambient lighting, provides overall diffused illumination. Ceiling lights and wall sconces are good examples of the types of fixtures that can typically provide general lighting. Post-and-rail lighting may also satisfy this function, but space the fixtures evenly around the deck for the best advantage.

Task lighting . . . illuminates a specific area or activity. As long as the weather permits, you'll want to use your outdoor room during the evening as well as on sunny summer days. That means you'll need good task lighting for an outdoor food-preparation and cooking area. Keep task lights on a switch that you can control separately from other types of outdoor light sources. Flood mounts or cylinder lights, which are typically used for general lighting, can accommodate task-lighting needs because they help to focus and direct light beams. ✱

1. Small path lights were added along the posts on this walkway for safety and to create focal points around the garden at night. **2.** On wide stairs, install lighting flush into the center of each riser to provide adequate illumination.

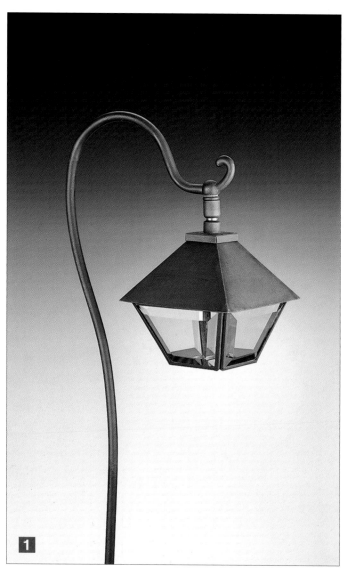

Accent lighting . . . high-lights elements in your landscape. It creates ambience and helps integrate the garden with the deck. Conventional low-voltage floodlights are excellent for creating effects such as wall grazing, silhouetting, and uplighting. ✦

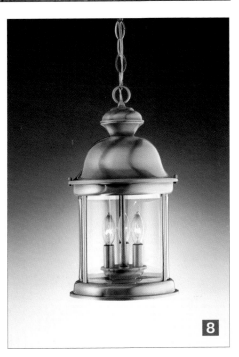

There are many types of decorative path lighting. **1.** This lantern-style fixture comes in antique bronze. **2.** Flame-tip bulbs bring a vintage look to traditional brass post lamps. **3.** Frosted glass diffuses the light from this iron fixture. **4.** You can aim spotlights to show off your garden. **5.** Modular path lights can either be mounted on stakes and moved easily or permanently attached to railings or posts. **6.** "Brick lights" are the size of a standard brick; the louver cover directs the beam of light downward. **7.** This classic carriage-style post lamp has a verdigris finish. **8.** A lantern hangs nicely over outdoor tables for added illumination. **9.** Spread lights are coated with a white finish to maximize the reflection of light.

DESIGN TIP

Use lighting to create decorative shadows. For interesting, undefined shadows, set lights at ground level aiming upward in front of a shrub or tree that is close to a wall. For silhouetting, place lights directly behind a plant or garden statue that is near a wall. In both cases, using a wide beam will increase the effect.

1. Combine the interior lights of your house with outdoor fixtures for dramatic effects. They could easily illuminate the deck and add exterior lighting for safety, especially near water. 2. Electrical outlets for decks are usually built into the side of the house to take advantage of existing wiring. 3. While wiring your deck, consider including telephone wires if you plan on using your notebook computer outside. 4. Some railings feature a cavity that allows you to run wire through them. 5. Connecting outdoor speakers to your indoor stereo system is a perfect way to add music for parties. 6. Protect all electrical outlets from the elements with a standard cover when not in use.

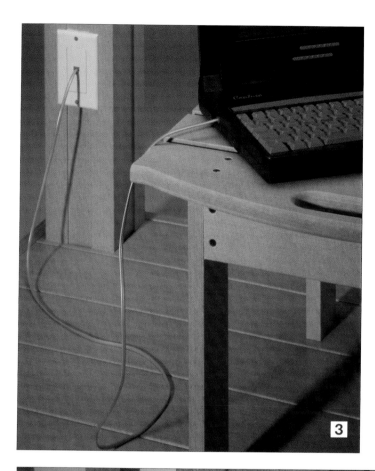

Furniture

Transform a simple deck into stylish,

comfortable living space

with furniture...

that's practical and good looking. Built-in seating and storage, constructed from the same material used to build the deck, is an option. But even if you include it in your plans, you'll probably need a few freestanding pieces as well. These may be simply a table and chairs or an entire ensemble of dining and side tables, plus perhaps a beverage trolley, easy chairs, and at least one chaise longue. Whatever your needs, here are a few things to know before you shop.

Today's furniture manufacturers are blurring the line between indoor and outdoor pieces. Both in terms of style and materials, a table or chair that was once thought suitable only for outside use may be perfectly at home indoors as well. The same is true for using indoor furniture in outdoor living spaces that are protected. In any case, comfort and durability have to be your main

This inviting chair, with its relaxed shape and beautiful wooden details, is perfect for sunning or snoozing on a deck by the sea.

considerations for choosing any outdoor pieces. Because they must endure the assaults of sun, rain, and sometimes salty sea air, outdoor furnishings require regular maintenance and refurbishing. How much depends upon the material, fabric, and protective finishes and coatings. Only you can be the judge of how much time you can devote to care, so keep this in mind when making your selection.

If the furniture has to stay outside year-round, it will take an even harder beating. Do you have space to store it over the winter months? If you're tight on space, buy lightweight collapsible pieces that you can fold up or stack out of the way easily. But remember, they can blow away if they're left out in a windy storm. Still, folding tables and chairs are practical, especially if you need extra seating and tables on occasion.

Another important issue is quality. Just as you would examine a piece of furniture for inside your home, carefully look over any pieces you're thinking of buying.

Shake the furniture to check for sturdiness, inspect the joints, and be sure that there are no protruding fasteners or jagged edges. Although high-quality pieces usually come with a higher price tag, they'll last in the long run.

Specifications

Generally, outdoor furniture is made of wood, metal, plastic or resin, or reed. Plastic or resin furniture is often lightweight, but metal and wood pieces are stronger and, coated with a protective finish, can tough-out the winter months outdoors. Unless cushions are covered in a waterproof, mildew-resistant fabric, they require storage when not in use.

An average table is 32 inches high, but countertop-height (36 inches) and bar-height (40 inches) are options. Like tables, outdoor chairs come in different heights: dining (17 inches high), counter (24 inches), and bar (30 inches). Before you buy a chair, be sure it's comfortable and check the width of the seat. Chairs usually range from 23 to 26 inches wide; chaise longues are 26 to 27 inches wide. Most settees, benches, swings, and gliders are 45 to 78 inches wide.

Cushion seating has a frame that can accommodate upholstered pads. Choose coated fabrics that hold up against the elements. Check for fillings that drain water quickly and maintain their shape. It is a good idea to have cushion storage nearby for days when inclement weather threatens. Large plastic storage chests are suitable for this purpose — and can double as emergency seating.

Sling seating features one continuous piece of woven fabric that forms the back and seat. Use it with or without a cushion. The woven seat can be left out in the rain because it dries quickly, but you may have to store the cushions. Sling seating is usually sun resistant; plasticizers help it hold its shape after repeated use. Most sling seating is replaceable — a saving because you can keep the frame of the chair.

Strap seating has closely placed bands of plastic pinned horizontally across the bottom and back of the frame. These bands range in thickness from 1 to 2 inches and can alternate in color. Typically, strap seating is only used on chairs or chaise longues, rarely on large pieces like settees. It is favored for poolside locations because it dries quickly.

Canvas seating is typically for director's chairs. It is durable, even without weather-resistant coatings, but it should be protected from the sun. However, you can replace the canvas once it is worn.

Vinyl mesh seating is practical for portable beach chairs. It is not a good option for decks because it cannot take the wear and tear of everyday use and will last only two to three summers.

Accessories

Portable bar and serving carts can be quickly set up anywhere your guests are. Carts with wheels are easy to move, and many come with coolers for cold beverages. Stackable matching bar stools are also available. If you're not putting in an outdoor kitchen or bar, these items are handy to have.

Here, a wicker chair with over-stuffed cushions provides a comfortable outdoor reading spot. Store fabric cushions during wet weather.

1. The natural look of these chairs blends well with the outdoor environment. **2.** This simple chair pad doesn't obscure the chair's unique twig frame. **3.** Weather-resistant cushions plump up the seat and back of this chair. **4.** Nestled in a deck corner, a wicker chair with warm coloring beckons passersby from the cool green foliage.

STYLE TIP

Mix-and-match table tops, frames, and legs are stylish. Combine materials such as glass, metal, wood, and mosaic tiles.

Reed furniture . . .

comes in wicker, rattan, or bamboo. Favored for its decorative appeal and comfort, reed furniture needs some protection from the elements if it is to last. For easy care, check out synthetic look-alikes. ✪

3

4

1. A pair of reed chaise longues enhances the tropical atmosphere. 2. When selecting outdoor furniture with attached fabric (especially a darker color), be sure that the fabric is fade-resistant. 3. The sleek lines of these wooden chaise longues bespeak contemporary sophistication. 4. Note how this striped cushion commands attention: chairs swathed in bold stripes instantly become deck focal points.

1

Resin furniture . . . is
made of molded plastic. Most
resin pieces are quite affordable, but lacquered resin with
brass fittings is a high-end
item. Resin doesn't corrode
and cleans easily, but a
scratched finish cannot be
repaired. Lacquered resin can
be touched up, however. ✿

2

1. Alfresco dining can be elegant, even with simple furniture, when it's set with glass, china, fruit, and flowers. 2. A wheeled serving cart is a practical addition to any deck. 3. Adirondack chairs, with their relaxed style and wide arms, are the mainstay of many decks. 4. Here, a generously sized side table puts all the necessities—food, beverages, and more—within easy reach.

STYLE TIP

Buy multipurpose outdoor furniture pieces. One type of resin chair that's on the market converts easily into a chaise longue. Just slide out the attachment stored underneath the seat. Don't overlook a particular piece's versatility. For example, an ottoman can be used as a small table, for seating, or as a footrest. Benches with lidded seats make excellent storage places for everything from tableware to cushions, gardening tools, charcoal, and seasoned wood chips.

1. Experience plush comfort, from head to toe, on cushions that cleverly disguise modest metal frames. **2.** Here, a metal and glass dining set is a practical yet decorative deck accessory that doesn't require much care. **3.** You can easily restyle a large metal baker's rack to serve as shelving for a profusion of potted plants.

Metal furniture . . .

is made from wrought or cast iron, aluminum, or steel. Aluminum is the affordable option and comes in many styles, but steel and iron offer durability and are good for windy locations. Rust is a problem for steel and iron; aluminum can bend. Check welds for a smooth seam. ✪

1. A diminutive chair actually serves here as a stylish drink holder. **2.** A duo of simple but sturdy chairs, matched by a table with handles, overlook a view of the backyard. **3.** Who wouldn't be tempted to sneak a swing in this suspended chair, complete with canopied protection from the sun and rain? **4.** This attractive contoured chair offers subtle lumbar support as part of its design. **5.** This chair reveals contours similar to the one above, but in a simpler form. **6.** The ever-popular folding director's chair is a staple of many decks. **7.** This contemporary chair, with its sturdy webbed construction, gains panache with scrolled arms and a verdigris finish. **8.** A casual chair, which matches the porch swing above, boasts clean lines, curved back legs for added stability, and the flourish of rolled arms.

3

4

5

6

7

8

1. Not to be outdone by any interior dining room, this deck is designed for elegant entertaining. **2.** You can stain any wooden furniture, such as this simple square side table, to match your deck. **3.** Both practical and convenient, this bench offers both wide side arms and a convenient back shelf. **4.** Note the high arms and sloped back of this chair, which make it perfect for relaxation. **5.** At first glance this table might seem plain, but its long, wooden planks showcase the handsome grain and finish. **6.** Whimsical curved arms add interest to this rocker's straightforward design. **7.** The variously stained, vertical wooden strips of the seat and back counterpoint this divan's strong horizontal line.

Wood furniture . . .

is typically made of oak, pine, cedar, redwood, or an exotic wood, such as teak. It blends well with almost any setting and is durable, but it does require more care to keep it sturdy and handsome. Check for solid, well crafted joints and a smooth, splinter-free finish. ⊙

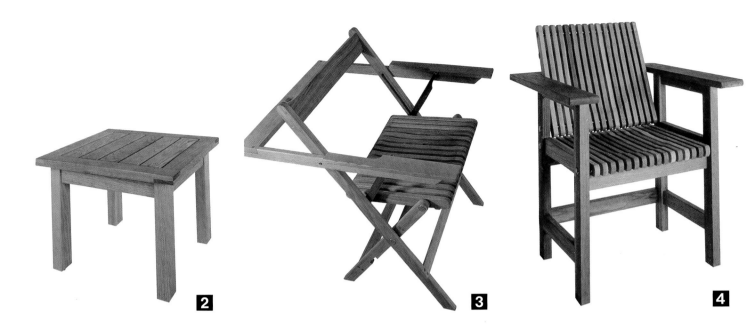

2

3

4

5

6

7

Cooking and Entertaining

As the trend toward outdoor entertaining gains

popularity, many people are setting up complete,

permanent outdoor cooking centers...

which often become the focus of their decks. Others content themselves with a simple grill. In either case, practical planning makes outdoor cooking efficient and more enjoyable, whether it is for everyday family meals or for a host of guests.

Decide exactly what features you want in the outdoor kitchen area. If you prefer to keep it simple with just a grill, you'll still have some decisions to make. Do you want a charcoal, gas, or electric unit? A charcoal grill is the least expensive option; a natural gas grill will cost you the most because it must be professionally installed. (Check with your local building department beforehand. Some locali-

Dining alfresco can be informal and elegant with pretty linens and place settings. Fresh flowers always lend beauty to the table.

ties will require a permit or may not allow this installation.) Extra features and accessories, such as rotisseries, woks, burners, smoke ovens, and warming racks increase the cost, too. Just remember: if you intend to locate the grill in a wooden enclosure, choose an insulated model that is designed for combustible applications.

In addition to a grill, do you want an elaborate setup with a sink, countertop, or a refrigerator? If so, these amenities will need protection from the elements. However, some refrigerators designed specifically for outdoor use can withstand harsh weather conditions. These high-end units are vented from the front and can be built-in or freestanding on casters. Typically, outdoor refrigerators are countertop height (often the same size as standard wine chilling units that mount underneath a kitchen countertop) and have shelving for food trays or drinks and in-door storage for condiments. Outdoor refrigerators intended strictly for cold beer storage come with a tap and can accommodate a half-keg.

More Entertainment Options

Do you entertain frequently? Think about including a custom-designed wet bar and countertop in your plans. Besides a sink, the unit can offer enclosed storage for beverages, ice, and glasses, and the countertop will be handy for serving or buffets. But if you can't handle the expense, consider a prefabricated open-air wet bar. It can be portable or built-in. Some portable wet-bars feature: a sink that you can hook up to the house plumbing or a garden hose (with a filter), ice bins with sliding lids, sectioned compartments for garnishes, a speed rail for bottles, and a beverage-chilling well. Deluxe models may come with extra shelves and side-mounted food warmers.

Practical Advantages

Integrating a cooking center with your deck provides easy access to the kitchen indoors. Remember, elaborate outdoor kitchens require gas, electricity, and plumbing; it is easier and less expensive to run those lines when the cooking area isn't at the other end of the yard. However, you'll have to carefully plan the cooktop so that it isn't too close to the house and so that the heat and smoke are directed away from seating areas.

In general, when arranging any outdoor cooking area, be sure that all accouterments — including serving platters, insulated mitts, basting brushes, spatulas, forks and knives, and long-handled tongs — are readily at hand

for the cook. And don't forget to plan enough surface room for setting down a tray of spices, condiments, sauces, and marinade or swiftly unloading a plate of hot grilled meats or vegetables. Because you'll have to juggle both uncooked and cooked foods, a roll-around cart may suffice. For safety's sake, always keep the pathway from the kitchen to the outdoor cooking area clear, and as a precaution, keep a fire extinguisher nearby.

Any outdoor countertop should be able to withstand varying weather conditions. Rain, snow, and bright sunlight will pit and rot some materials, so choose carefully. Tile, concrete, or natural stone (such as slate) are the best options. Concrete can be tinted and inlaid for decorative effect but, like stone, it is porous and must be sealed. Avoid a surface laminate unless it's for use in a well-protected area because exposure to the weather causes the layers to separate. Solid-surfacing material is more durable, but it's better left to a sheltered location. Think twice about using teak or other decay-resistant woods for a countertop. Although these woods weather handsomely, they are not sealed against bacteria, so you can't expose them directly to food. If you do select a wooden countertop, insert a tray or plate under any uncooked meats and vegetables.

Decay-resistant woods such as redwood, cedar, teak, or mahogany are, however, good choices for outdoor cabinetry. Other types of wood will have to be sealed and stained or painted. Another option is oriented-strand board (OSB). Made of bonded wood fiber, oriented-strand board is also weatherproof.

You can set up an impromptu brunch anywhere on the deck. Lightweight portable furniture and a few potted plants create instant atmosphere.

Grill Checklist

Look for these important features:

- An electronic push-button ignition. It starts better because it emits a continuous spark; knob igniters emit two to three sparks per turn.

- Insulated handles. These are convenient because they don't get hot. Otherwise you'll need a grilling mitt to protect yourself from burns when using the controls.

- Easy access to the propane tank. Some gas grills feature tilt-out bins, which make connecting and changing the tank a snap.

A grill cover should fit snugly. Some covers have adjustable lids, which allow airflow so that food cooks slowly and evenly.

Adjustable controls allow you to control the heat level of burners.

Side burners let you sauté toppings, simmer sauces, or fry side dishes. A side burner can come with a protective cover that also doubles as an extra landing surface for utensils.

A towel hook is a useful detail on a grill. Check for other extras, such as utility hooks for utensils, condiment compartments on side shelves, or warming racks.

Casters make the grill portable so that it is easy to reposition at your convenience. Keep in mind that a large stainless-steel grill can be as heavy as 230 pounds.

Selecting a Grill

It's not the size of the grill that counts; it's whether you have the space on the deck to accommodate it. Measure the intended cooking area before shopping, and take those measurements with you to the store or home center. Depending upon your budget, you may also want to consider one of the high-end units that luxury kitchen appliance manufacturers have introduced into the marketplace. They have lots of features and are built to last, but they are expensive and must be professionally installed. Serious cooks like them.

Think about the grill's location in relationship to the traffic, dining, and lounging zones. How far away will the grill be from the house? If your space is limited or if you expect a lot of activity — large crowds or kids underfoot — you may have to relegate the cooking area to someplace close, but not on the deck itself.

Also consider how many people you typically cook for. Check out the grill's number of separate heating zones (there should be at least two) before buying it. If you have a large family or entertain frequently, you'll need a grill that can accommodate large quantities or different types of food at the same time.

Grill Features

Because you'll probably be using your new grill more often and with a greater variety of foods, buy one that has some important basic options. Are there any special features that you'd like with your grill? Extra burners, a rotisserie, a warming rack, or a smoker? What do you like

to cook? Today, you can prepare more than hamburgers and barbecued chicken on your grill. In fact, tasty, healthy grilled food is popular year-round and so you may be cooking outdoors from spring through late fall.

Many models now come with two burners, but larger ones have more. The burners should have adjustable temperature controls that will allow you to set the heat at high, medium, or low. Ideally, a unit should sustain an even cooking temperature and provide at least 33,000 Btu (British thermal units, the measurement for heat output) when burners are set on high. A slow-roasting setting is optional on some models. If you enjoy sauces, make sure your grill comes with adjustable side burners, which can accommodate pots and sauce pans.

Fireplaces & Fire Pits

As an alternative to grills, you may want to consider a fireplace or a fire pit. Although neither one has the cooking flexibility of a high-end grill, it will provide heat, extending the use of your deck as the evening becomes cooler. Plus, the glow of a fireplace or fire pit is sure to create an inviting, cozy atmosphere on any deck.

Fireplaces and fire pits are suitable for ground-level decks only, and the surround and chimney should be constructed of masonry. Today, you can purchase a clay fire pit that rests on a metal stand. Before installing an outdoor fireplace or pit, check with your building inspector regarding regulations and permits. Also, if you plan on buying a portable pit, be sure to follow any safety precautions suggested by the manufacturer.

1. Treat your guests to a great view, if your deck offers one. Bring out a table from indoors and set up a spot for drinks. **2.** Comfortable furniture is always inviting and an important element of your party plan.

A conversation area apart from
the cooking zone permits
the owners of this deck to enjoy
the air away from smoke and heat.

1. A simple bench and a few chairs create a pleasant place for outdoor snacks. **2.** Without an outdoor kitchen, the owners of this deck set up the dining area just outside the back door for convenience.

1. This deck boasts a fully equipped kitchen. **2.** Brick surrounds this built-in fire pit. **3.** A fireplace can be an alternative or an addition to a grill. **4.** It's important to include countertops or other surfaces next to the grill. Use them for platters of hot food, for marinades, or to keep utensils nearby.

A Self-Quiz

If you're considering an outdoor kitchen, here are some questions to ask yourself:

- How much time will you spend in it? Will you use it during the daytime and/or evening?

- About how many people will you be cooking for?

- What types of food will you cook? Will you need any special accessories? Will you need refrigeration?

- Will you need additional outdoor lighting and electrical outlets?

- Do you have a protected spot in which to locate an outdoor kitchen?

- Is this location near the house so that it will be easy to extend the utility lines and plumbing?

SAFETY TIP

Hoses on gas grills can develop leaks. To check the hose on your gas grill, brush soapy water over it. If you see any bubbles, turn off the gas valve and disconnect the tank. Then replace the hose.

1. This market umbrella gives diners a respite from the hot sun. 2. Here, fire in another form adds ambiance to an enclosed deck. Everyday candles are a lovely, inexpensive source of deck lighting. 3. When dining outdoors, it helps to have places to set out the food, such as on this tiered serving rack. 4. It's like meals on wheels. This portable grill moves easily over a deck or patio. 5. An outdoor refrigerator is about the size of a wine cooler.

Shade

Every deck can benefit from some shade or covering for at least part of the day. . .

but ardent sun worshippers may want nothing more than an umbrella overhead. Most people require an area with more covering, however. Coverings also increase your usable time on a deck because they provide protection from the weather. Before you decide what kind of covering you need, check the location of the deck and the time of day when the sun is strongest on the space.

A *south-facing deck* gets direct sunlight for most of the day, so it will require maximum protection in the form of a roof or awning to make it comfortable. An *east-facing* deck gets early morning sunlight, while a *west-facing* deck will be hot and sunny in the afternoon. If a covering is necessary—and it may not be depending on what time of day you use the space—retractable awnings are good for east-facing decks because they are easy to roll up when the deck cools down. Think about protection from horizontal

Trees shade this deck for most of the day. However, an umbrella can be used whenever it's necessary to cover sunny spots.

rays for west-facing decks because the low-lying sun in the afternoon can stream under any covering, causing glare. Try hanging roll-up shades with bamboo or plastic quills to cut the glare. You can usually order awnings with side screens for this purpose. Because a *north-facing* deck receives only indirect natural light and tends to be cool, it won't need a covering for shade, but you may want to consider protection from the weather.

Permanent Coverings

A permanent covering defines a section of your deck, making it stand out. Whenever possible, it should blend with the architectural style of your house. Fortunately, there are a number of attractive options from which to choose, including pergolas, gazebos, and solid roofing. A *pergola* is a framed structure with spaced rafters or a latticework top. The open design of a pergola is favored for decks because it provides light shade while remaining airy. A pergola is more than a functional addition: it is a decorative one, too. The spacing and pattern of the rafters create playful shadows that enhance the appeal of your deck. A pergola can be attached to the house or left freestanding, and it is relatively affordable to build. Exposure to the elements is the one drawback to a pergola. It won't keep your deck dry nor will it fully protect the area from sunlight.

Unlike a pergola, a *gazebo* is usually independent of the house, but it can be incorporated into a section of the deck. A gazebo is a framed structure with a peaked roof that is usually circular or octagonal in shape. It is often adorned with fretwork and turned post railings, which give a gazebo a romantic Victorian-style air. Built-in benches make a gazebo more useful, but you can also set up a freestanding table and chairs in the center. To tie the gazebo into your overall scheme, choose a roofing material that matches that of the house.

Solid roofing can range from a classic shingled roof with gutters to a light covering of woven reed to corrugated plastic panels. A roof provides the most protection and truly becomes integrated with the house. It does, however, block light to the house and can add significantly to the cost of your deck. Make sure the roof is built to withstand snow loads if you live in a four-season climate. In more-temperate climates, it is common to build a frame and cover the top with woven reeds, such as bamboo. The texture of the reed covering adds an exotic look to your deck and filters light softly. It gives some protection from rain, but because the covering is woven, water will leak through. Corrugated plastic panels are solid protection from the weather and allow some light through because the panels are not completely opaque —

a desirable feature if the covering is attached to the house. The frame holding the plastic panels has to be angled so that water will run off and not build up in the grooves. Plastic panels can fade and yellow over time.

Fabric Coverings

Fabric coverings consist of weather-resistant material supported by a frame made of aluminum, steel, or wood. Awnings are the best known in this category and can be retractable or stationary. Shade cloth is gaining popularity but performs better in warm locales. Sun tents and umbrellas are portable and easy to set up anywhere.

Frame awnings use a stationary system of steel supports (both vertical and horizontal) to hold a canvas awning in place. The canvas is attached with lacing or a rotary tension bar. If you live in a mild zone, this type of awning can remain out year-round. Retractable awnings are designed with a folding-arm frame that doesn't require vertical supports. (Older systems use cable or chain mechanisms.) Some awnings are manually operated; others are motorized. Any awning system is an investment, but shop around because prices do vary. Keep in mind that extras, like wind sensors that pull in retractable awnings when the wind velocity gets too high, will increase the costs.

The canvas used for awnings is a tightly woven cotton fabric — usually army duck — that comes in various weights. Like most outdoor fabrics, it can contain water-repellent and other coatings that make it resistant to ultraviolet light damage, mildew, or fire. There are also synthetic fabrics that

In a stand, the aluminum pole of this scallop-edged umbrella can handle the wind and weather at this seaside location.

1. A portable market umbrella. **2.** Use it to shade the table. **3.** As the sun shifts during the day, move the umbrella to another spot, as needed. **4.** To prevent costly damage, purchase wind sensors for retractable awnings that will automatically pull them in if gusts go over 50 mph.

are equally as capable and enduring as canvas but which have the look of natural fiber.

Shade cloth is a woven fabric that is durable for outdoor use. It comes in different weaves that provide varying amounts of shade—from light coverage to almost complete opacity. It's usually green or black and hangs on a wooden frame via hooks and grommets. You can hang strips of shade cloth across the frame like a horizontal curtain by using wire cables and clasps. The cloth can be adjusted anywhere along the wire, allowing you to control the amount of light exposure. This is a less-expensive alternative to an awning.

A *sun tent* is a movable structure on a lightweight aluminum frame that can be staked in the ground or tied to a deck. A synthetic fabric is stretched over the frame, creating the tent. Sun tents are convenient because they're easy to move and don't have to be put away until the cold weather comes. If you live in a windy location, be sure the sun tent is securely fastened so that it doesn't blow over. A sun tent is one of the less-expensive options, but remember that it isn't as durable as an awning.

Umbrellas are the ubiquitous summertime covering and the perfect supplement to a deck. Sun lovers may find that an umbrella is the only coverage that they want on their decks. Traditionally, umbrellas featured aluminum poles and spokes, but upscale market umbrellas now sport finished wood supports with brass fittings or powder-coated aluminum in different colors. There is an endless choice in fabrics (usually canvas or vinyl coated), patterns, and colors. You can even order custom-designed umbrellas to match your deck's décor.

1. Shade can be decorative; standard umbrellas come in a variety of colors and patterns to match your deck furniture, or you can have one custom-made to meet your needs. 2. Canvas awnings provide complete shade for those sensitive to the sun. Like umbrellas, they come in many colors and patterns. Stripes are classic. 3. A decorative finial was added to the top of this plain umbrella to give it personality.

(**DESIGN TIP**)

Awnings come in bright colors. As light filters through, it will cast a hue to anything under the deck. Warm colors, such as red or pink, will create a rosy glow; cool colors, such blues or greens, will enhance the shade.

Choosing Colors

When choosing a color for your awning, instead of blending with the landscape or house, you can pick one that contrasts its surroundings. This will draw attention to a handsome deck.

1. Decorative awnings can also be practical, such as this one that prevents the hot sun from beating through the window. **2.** An awning makes a deck usable whatever the weather by offering protection from the rain and buffering the wind. **3.** If the commercial awnings don't match your style, you can improvise shading with the right fabrics. This covering was made from canvas that was treated with a mildew-resistant coating.

PASOLINI REQUIEM

3

1. Before choosing an umbrella, decide how much shade you would like for your deck. Standard umbrellas usually measure from $7^1/_2$ to $8^1/_2$ feet in diameter, while market umbrellas are slightly larger at 8 to 10 feet in diameter. **2.** Using more than one umbrella allows for ample shade. **3.** Standard umbrellas are sometimes referred to as drape umbrellas because of the hanging border that is scalloped or left straight. **4.** As you plan for shade, remember that the sun will affect your deck differently during the four seasons. For example, the angle of the sun will be lower in the winter than in the summer, changing the light and shade patterns.

4

Adding Water

There's nothing like the sight and

sound of water to lend

a refreshing quality to . . .

your deck. In fact, water can be a dynamic element in both the deck's design and its function. It can be in the form of one of the ultimate outdoor luxuries — a pool, spa, or hot tub — or in a water feature such as a fountain, waterfall, or pond. In any case, because of the relaxing qualities of water, you should consider integrating some form of it into your plans.

Planning a deck near a pool requires taking the size and shape of the pool into consideration. In most cases, the pool will be a focal point in a landscape, so the design of

the surrounding deck, including the flooring patterns, materials, and other details, can either enhance or detract from

Because water is a natural element that people are drawn to, it can be the perfect unobtrusive addition to your deck. For instance, this pool's dark lining easily blends in with the beauty of the landscape.

its appeal. Aside from looks, think about how a pool deck will function. For sunbathing? Exercising? Entertaining? All three?

Another way to enjoy water with your deck is with a soothing spa. Requiring less space than a pool, a spa uses hydrojets to move heated water. One type, a hot tub, is a barrel-like enclosure filled with water. It may or may not have jets and usually features an adjustable but simple bench. It offers a deeper soak — as much as 4 feet — than other types of spas, and many homeowners like the look of an aboveground hot tub's wood exterior. The tub comes with a vinyl or plastic liner.

A built-in spa is set into a deck or the ground (in-ground). It can be acrylic, or it can be constructed of poured concrete, gunite, or shotcrete. A spa can stand alone or be integrated with a large pool.

A portable spa is a completely self-contained unit that features an acrylic spa shell, a wooden surround, and all of the equipment needed to heat and move the water. A portable spa costs less than an in-ground unit, and it runs on a standard 120-volt circuit. You can locate a portable spa on a concrete slab in your yard. But you can also install one on the deck. Just make sure there is proper structural support underneath the deck to sustain the additional weight of the unit, the water, and bathers. Check with the local building inspector regarding any code regulations that may apply.

1

GARDEN TIP

To keep water clear in ponds or small water gardens, use aquatic plants. Miniature water lilies are just right for tub cultivation.

1. Just as mirrors make a small area feel spacious indoors, a reflecting basin can do the same for your deck outdoors. **2.** This built-in spa was sunk into a partially covered nook to one side of the main deck. Lattice fencing and plantings add privacy.

1. Reserve an out-of-the-way corner for a spa. 2. Decking around an in-ground pool feels natural under bare feet. 3. This spa deck combination is the ideal at-home getaway. The use of stone and redwood makes an interesting design. 4. Color and shape work together to make this deck a visual treat.

Water Features

Water features create the ambiance of a soothing oasis on a deck. A water-filled urn becomes a mirror that reflects the sky — making a small deck look larger. Fish flashing in an ornamental pool add color and act as a focal point for a deck with no view. A water fountain introduces a pleasant rhythmical sound that helps drown out the background noises of traffic and nearby neighbors.

3

4

1. The owners of this deck have the best of both worlds. The pool looks like an ornamental pond, yet it is a fully functional swimming area. **2.** Rather than take up a lot of deck space with the stairs, these homeowners decided to curve the stairs around the side of the deck, creating a corner perfect for a built-in spa. **3.** If you know that you will be moving in the near future, a portable spa, as seen here, can move with you to your new home.

Resources

Planning

DeckWeb *is an Internet site that provides information on deck design, building, finishing, and furnishing. The site also offers directories of product manufacturers and deck designers. The DeckForum Q&A message board allows homeowners to post questions for professional deck builders and interested do-it-yourselfers.*

www.deckweb.com

Sierra On-line's *SierraHome division produces computer programs for home design, landscaping, and gardening. Their Web site offers building and gardening how-to advice.*

3060 139th Ave. SE

Suite 500

Bellevue, WA 98005

Phone: 800-757-7707

www.sierrahome.com

Materials

APA-The Engineered Wood Association (APA) *is a nonprofit trade association whose U.S. and Canadian members produce a variety of engineered wood products. Primary functions include quality inspection and product promotion. Write for free brochures.*

P.O. Box 11700

Tacoma, WA 98411

www.apawood.org

Boundary Fence & Railing *manufactures and distributes a variety of fences and railings. The firm does its own fence weaving and either vinyl- or powder-coating. They offer many types of chain-link mesh, hard-to-get fittings, ornamental wood gate hardware, over 150 professional fence tools, razor coil, and a line of 100% PVC fencing.*

Phone: (800) 628-8928

www.boundary-fences.com

California Redwood Association, *a nonprofit trade association, offers extensive technical information about redwood, including grade distinctions, structural applications, and finishing characteristics. The Association also has design and how-to help for consumers. Write for a free brochure.*
405 Enfrente Dr., Suite 200
Novato, CA 94949
www.calredwood.org

The Flood Company *is a 150-year-old, family-owned corporation that makes a variety of paint-related products, including penetrating stains, sealers, wood renewers, and cleaners. The company Web site offers a full rundown of products, information on application tools, and a store locator.*
Phone: (800) 321-3444
www.floodco.com

Hickson Corporation *manufactures pressure-treated wood for decks, landscaping, walkways, gazebos, fences, and picnic tables. For information and building plans, such as "How to Build the Best Deck" and "How to Build Backyard Projects," call or visit its Web site.*
1955 Lake Park Dr., Suite 250,
Smyrna, GA 30080
Phone: (770) 801-6600
www.hickson.com

Kroy Building Products *is a leading manufacturer of vinyl decks, deck and porch railings, fences, and other vinyl products. Free catalogs, technical information, and specifications are available.*
P.O. Box 636
York, NE 68467
Phone: 800-933-5769
www.kroybp.com

Southern Pine Council *is a nonprofit trade promotion group supported by manufacturers of southern pine lumber. Construction details and building tips, complete project plans, and other helpful information are described in a free catalog.*

P.O. Box 641700

Kenner, LA 70064

www.southernpine.com

Timber Holdings LTD. *imports exotic outdoor hardwoods including ipé and jarrah under the brand name Iron Wood, which the company says offers unique resistance to decay and insects. Call for a free catalog and deck project brochure.*

2400 West Cornell

Milwaukee, WI 53209

Phone: 414-445-8989

www.ironwoods.com

TimberTech Limited *products combine recycled wood and polymers to form complete deck systems that include railings, fascia boards, and a variety of planking. Call for a free catalog.*

P.O. Box 182880

Columbus, OH 43218

Phone: 800-307-7780

www.timbertech.com

Trex *is a leading manufacturer of recycled wood and plastic decking materials. Free literature, a materials guide, and design ideas are available. Complete service and a retailer guide are provided.*

www.trex.com

U.S. Plastic Lumber *manufactures 100% recycled plastic deck systems and wood-plastic composite systems sold under the Carefree and SmartDeck brand names. They also produce recycled plastic timbers and furnishings.*

2600 W. Roosevelt Road

Chicago, IL 60608

Phone: 312-491-2500

www.usplasticlumber.com

Western Wood Products Association (WWPA) *establishes standards and levels of quality for western lumber and related products in western softwood species. Technical information is available via fax or on their Web site.*

522 SW 5th Avenue

Suite 500

Portland, OR 97204-2122

Phone: (503) 224-3930 / Fax: (503) 224-3934

www.wwpa.org

Furnishings

AGI Group *offers a varied selection of patio umbrellas and fine teak outdoor furnishings. The Web site links to several retailers and on-line catalogs for efficient service and shopping.*

1951 Porter Lake Drive, Suite E

Sarasota, FL 34240

Phone: 941-377-5336

Fax: 941-377-6516

www.shuttertime.com

Anchor Industries, Inc. *produces a comprehensive line of custom awnings, pool covers, canopies, and other sewn and heat-sealed products for residential use. The Web site provides on-line shopping and a product guide.*

1100 Burch Drive

Evansville, IN 47725

Phone: 800-255-5552

Fax: 812-867-0547

www.anchorinc.com

Campania International, Inc. *offers an exceptional collection of planters, statuary, and garden ornaments in fine cast stone, polyethylene, and terra-cotta. The Web site displays a selection of pieces. Request a catalog.*

401 Fairview Avenue

Quakertown, PA 18951

Phone: 215-538-1106

Fax: 215-538-2522

www.camapaniainternational.com

Frontgate *offers everything you need to know about its complete line of grills and accessories, including detailed specifications and construction drawings. Browse its outdoor furniture catalog featuring a distinctive collection of casual outdoor furnishings and accessories created by the world's finest furniture makers.*

5566 West Chester Road

West Chester, OH 45069

Phone: 800-626-6488

Fax: 800-436-2105

www.frontgate.com

Malibu Intermatic Incorporated *offers an impressive assortment of garden and landscaping lighting solutions. The Web site presents different lighting scenarios and free literature.*
Intermatic Plaza
Spring Grove, IL 60081-9698
Phone: 815-675-2321
www.intermatic.com

Progress Lighting *produces a wide array of indoor and outdoor lighting fixtures. A catalog and a list of retailers is available through the Web site.*
101 Corporate Drive, Suite L
Spartanburg, SC 29303-5007
Phone: 864-599-6123
www.progresslighting.com

Telescope Casual Furniture, Inc. *produces a wide array of garden and deck furniture. Chairs, tables, and umbrellas are available in a myriad of styles and fabrics. The Web site provides a product and retail guide.*
85 Church St.
P.O. Box 299
Granville, NY 12832
Phone: 518-642-1100
Fax: 518-642-2536
www.telescopecasual.com

Fiskars *offers a wide selection of outdoor accessories. The Web site provides a fine selection of garden and deck furnishings as well as lawn and patio ornaments. The site will link you to various manufacturers and suppliers.*
636 Science Drive
Madison, WI 53711

Phone: 608-233-1649
Fax: 608-233-5321
www.fiskars.com

Kingsley~Bate Limited *is a leading retailer of outdoor solid teak furniture. An impressive line of benches, dining sets and lounging chairs can be viewed on the web site. They also supply a wide variety of lawn and garden accessories. Request a catalog, or a care and maintenance and retailer guide.*
5587-B Guinea Road
Fairfax, VA 22032
Phone: 703-978-7200
Fax: 703-978-7222
www.kingsleybate.com

Summit Furniture, Inc. *offers an extensive variety of teak chairs and outdoor dining sets.*
5 Harris Court #W
Monterey, CA
Phone: 831-375-7811

Grills & Appliances

Martin Industries, Inc. *produces a diverse line of Broilmaster standard and deluxe grills. The on-line page presents several models as well as custom grill specifications. Literature request provided.*

301 East Tennessee Street

Florence, AL 35630

Phone: 256-740-518

www.broilmaster.com

Weber-Stephen Products Co. *provides a fine selection gas and charcoal grills, plus a line of portables. The Web site will walk you through various lines as well as a product comparison. It also provides information on grilling accessories and a detailed buyers guide.*

200 East Daniels Road

Palatine, IL 60067-6266

Phone: 800-446-1071

Fax: 847-705-7971

www.weber.com

Sub-Zero *is the leading manufacturer of a complete line of stock and custom refrigeration units. The Web site offers step-by-step custom ideas as well as an impressive on-line product catalog. A distributor guide is also included.*

4717 Hammersley Road

Madison, WI 53711

Phone: 608-271-2233

www.sub-zero.com

Landscaping

Beckett Corporation *is a leader in the manufacturing of safe and environmentally sound underwater pumps for ponds and fountains. A visit to the Web site will help you configure a pump system to fit your needs.*

5931 Campus Circle Drive

Irving, TX 75063-2606

Phone: 1-888-BECKETT

www.beckettpumps.com

Cooperative State Research, Education, and Extension Services (CSREES) *offers educational outreach to people in a variety of subjects, among them agricultural and natural resources, through its extension agents, numerous publications, and Master Gardener phone information lines. A national directory of services is available in many public libraries and on the Web site listed below.*

U.S. Dept. of Agriculture, CSREES

Rm. 3328, South Bldg.

Washington, DC 20250-0907

www.reeusda.gov/1700/statepartners/usa.htm

Waterford Gardens *provides you with a complete and comprehensive guide to selecting the best aquatic plants and flowers for your individual needs. The on-line catalog carries a wide selection of lilies, lotuses, and marginal plants.*

74 East Allendale Road

Saddle River, NJ 07458

Phone: 201-327-0721

Fax: 201-327-0684

www.waterford-gardens.com

Glossary

Accent Lighting *Lighting that highlights a space or object to emphasize its character.*

Ambient Lighting *General illumination for an area, provided without a visible light source.*

Asymmetry *The balance between objects of different sizes formed by their placement or grouping. When the scale is correct, asymmetry can be as pleasing as symmetry, though it's more informal.*

Awning, Frame *The weather-resistant fabric of this type of awning is attached by lacing or a rotary tension bar to a frame made of aluminum, steel, or wood. The frame supports usually extend to the deck floor or are attached to the railings. Awnings can provide varying degrees of shade, depending on the weight of the canvas.*

Awning, Retractable *Retractable awnings have a folding-arm frame that doesn't require vertical supports. The awning moves in and out by a manual or motorized pulley system, and may be activated by a sensor when winds exceed 50 miles per hour.*

Backlighting *Illumination placed behind or to the side of an object. See "Silhouetting."*

Balance, in Design *Equilibrium of the forms in a defined area. Relationships between objects in balance seem natural and comfortable to the eye, and balanced relationships may be symmetrical or asymmetrical.*

Balusters *The vertical pieces, often made of 2x2 or 1x4, that fill in spaces between rail posts and provide a fence-like structure.*

Brick Lights *These lights are the size of a standard brick, and their louvered covers direct the beam of light downward. Install these unobtrusive fixtures in walls or near stairs and pathways.*

Building Codes *Municipal rules regulating safe building practices and procedures. Generally, the codes encompass structural, electrical, plumbing, and mechanical remodeling and new construction. Inspection may be required to ensure conformity to local codes.*

Building Permit *A license that authorizes construction on your home. Minor repairs and remodeling work usually do not call for a permit, but if the job consists of extending the water supply and drain, waste, vent system; adding an electrical circuit; or making structural changes to a building; a permit may be necessary.*

Built-In, Deck *Any element, such as a bench or planter, that is attached permanently to the deck.*

Cantilever *Construction that extends beyond its vertical support.*

Canvas Seating *A type of sturdy cotton that is typically used on director's chairs, canvas seating is durable, even without weather-resistant coatings. It will last longer if protected from the sun, but is easily replaced.*

Chaise Longue *A long chair with back support and a seat long enough for outstretched legs.*

Clearance *The amount of space between two fixtures or around furniture, the centerlines of two fixtures, or a fixture and an obstacle, such as a wall. Clearances may be mandated by codes.*

Cushion Seating *Cushion seating has a frame designed to accommodate upholstered pads. The fabric used for outdoor cushions should be treated to resist water, mildew, and sun.*

Decay-Resistant Woods *Woods such as redwood, cedar, teak, or mahogany, which are naturally resistant to rot.*

Diffused Light *Indirect or softly filtered light.*

Fascia *Facing that covers the exposed ends and sides of decking to create a finished appearance.*

Fire Pit *A built-in masonry well, typically built into the center of the deck, used to contain a fire.*

Floodlights *Outdoor lights with strong, bright beams used for security or to highlight an object.*

Focal Point *The dominant element in a space.*

Gazebo *A framed structure with a peaked roof that is usually circular or octagonal. A gazebo offers roofed protection from the rain and sun, and can stand alone or be built into the deck.*

Grade *The ground level. On-grade means at or on the natural ground level.*

Grill, Charcoal *A type of grill that uses charcoal to heat and cook food.*

Grill, Electric *A type of grill that requires an electrical outlet.*

Grill, Gas *A gas grill, which preheats for only about ten minutes, uses liquid propane (LP) or natural gas.*

Harmony, in Design *Design harmony is achieved when all elements relate pleasingly to one another, forming a complementary whole.*

Hot Tub *This barrel-like, water-filled enclosure may or may not have jets, and usually features a simple, adjustable bench. It offers a deeper soak than other types of spas (as high as 4 feet), and has an attractive wood exterior.*

Joist *A structural member, usually two-by lumber, commonly placed perpendicularly across beams to support deck boards.*

Lattice *A cross-pattern structure made of wood, metal, or plastic.*

Louvers *Horizontal slats, which may or may not be tiltable, that block or direct light.*

Low-Voltage Lighting *Low-voltage transformers convert 120-volt household current to 12 volts in order to power outdoor lighting.*

Matte Finish *A flat, nonreflective, nonglossy surface finish.*

Mediterranean Style *A European style influenced by warm-climate living. It uses natural materials of varying textures, such as painted ceramic tile, terra-cotta clay, stone, ironwork, and wood. The design as a whole often features terraces and an open floor plan that encourages air circulation.*

Metal Furniture *Metal furniture includes pieces wrought of cast iron, aluminum, or steel. Aluminum is affordable and comes in many styles, but can bend. Steel and iron are durable and stable in windy locations, but may rust.*

Path Lights *Path lights vary in style from utilitarian to decorative, but all provide safe, functional outdoor illumination. Although modular path lights are typically mounted on portable stakes, you can permanently attach them to railings or posts.*

Pergola *A framed structure with spaced rafters or a latticework top. Pergolas are favored for decks because they provide light shade while remaining airy. For more coverage, grow flowering vines over the pergola.*

Pressure-Treated Lumber *Wood that has had preservatives forced into it under pressure to repel rot and insects.*

Proportion *Proportion refers to the relationship of parts or objects to one another based on their size.*

Railing *Assembly made from balusters attached to rails and installed between posts as a safety barrier at the edge of a deck.*

Railing Cap *A horizontal piece of lumber laid flat on top of the post and top rail, covering the end grain of the post and providing a flat surface that is wide enough for setting down objects.*

Reed Furniture *Reed furniture commonly is made of wicker, rattan, or bamboo. While favored for its decorative appeal and comfort, reed furniture needs some protection from the elements.*

Resin Furniture *Inexpensive and made of molded plastic, resin furniture cleans easily and doesn't corrode.*

Credits

Page 1: *Photographer:* Philip Clayton-Thompson **page 2:** *Photographer:* Jessie Walker Associates **page 6:** *Photographer:* Brian Vanden Brink **page 8:** *Photographer:* Mark Samu **page 11:** *Photographer:* Brian Vanden Brink **page 12:** *Photographer:* Western Cedar Association **page 14:** *Photographer:* Brian Vanden Brink **page 15:** *Photographer:* Crandall & Crandall **page 16:** *Photographer: (top)* Dolores Z. Elliot; *(bottom)* The Flood Company **page 17:** *Photographer: (top)* California Redwood Association; *(bottom)* Dolores Z. Elliot **page 18:** *Photographer:* Derek Fell **page 19:** *Photographer: (top & bottom)* Crandall & Crandall **page 20:** *Photographer: (top)* Western Cedar Association; *(bottom left)* Derek Fell; *(bottom right)* Crandall & Crandall **page 21:** *Photographer: (top)* Crandall & Crandall; *(bottom)* Dolores Z. Elliot **page 22:** *Photographer: (top)* Trex Decks; *(bottom)* Timber Tech **page 23:** *Photographer: (all)* Trex Decks **page 24:** *Photographer:* California Redwood Association **page 26:** Southern Forest Product Association **page 27:** *Photographer:* Dolphin *Architect:* Walt Schlager **page 28:** *Photographer: (all)* Crandall & Crandall **page 29:** *Photographer:* Derek Fell **page 30:** *Photographer:* Michael Thompson **page 31:** *Photographer: (top)* Tim Street-Porter; *(bottom)* Michael Thompson **page 32:** *Photographer: (top)* Michael Thompson; *(bottom left)* Crandall & Crandall; *(bottom right)* Grey Crawford **page 33:** *Photographer: (all)* Crandall & Crandall **page 34:** *Photographer:* Crandall & Crandall **page 35:** *Photographer: (top)* California

Redwood Association; *(bottom)* Mark Lohman **page 36:** *Photographer:* Jessie Walker Associates **page 39:** *Photographer: (top left)* Michael Thompson; *(top right and center left)* Derek Fell; *(center right)* Crandall & Crandall; *(bottom left)* Mark Samu; *(bottom right)* Dolphin *Architects:* Walt Schlager **page 40:** *Photographer: (top)* Jessie Walker Associates; *(center left)* Crandall & Crandall; *(bottom)* Derek Fell **page 41:** *Photographer: (all)* Mark Samu **page 42:** *Photographer: (all)* Crandall & Crandall **page 43:** *Photographer: (top)* Jessie Walker Associates; *(bottom) Photographer:* Derek Fell *Designer:* Brickman Group **page 44:** *Photographer: (top)* Jessie Walker Associates; *(center)* Derek Fell; *(bottom left)* Mark Samu, courtesy of Hearst Specials; *(bottom right)* Crandall & Crandall **page 45:** *Photographer: (top)* Mark Samu; *(bottom)* Western Cedar Association **page 46:** *Photographer:* Crandall & Crandall **page 47:** *Photographer:* Mark Samu, courtesy of Hearst Specials **page 48:** *Photographer:* Smart Deck **page 51:** *Photographer:* Tim Street-Porter **page 52:** *Photographer: (top left and bottom)* Malibu Lighting/Intermatic; *(top right)* Michael Thompson **page 53:** *Photographer: (top)* H. Armstrong Roberts; *(bottom)* Malibu Lighting/Intermatic **page 54:** *Photographer:* Crandall & Crandall **page 55:** *Photographer:* Trex Decks **pages 56–57:** *Photographer: (all)* Progress Lighting **page 58:** *Photographer: (top)* Dolphin *Architects:* Walt Schlager; *(bottom)* Brian Vanden Brink **page 59:** *Photographer: (all)* Smart Deck **page 60:** *Photographer:* Mark Lohman **page 63:**

Photographer: Mark Lohman **page 64:** *Photographer: (top)* Mark Lohman; *(bottom)* Michael Thompson **page 65:** *Photographer: (top)* Sunbrella Fabrics; *(bottom)* Michael Thompson **page 66:** *Photographer:* Mark Lohman **page 67:** *Photographer: (top)* Jessie Walker Associates; *(center)* Summit Furniture; *(bottom)* Dolores Z. Elliot **page 68:** *Photographer: (top)* Steve Cridland; *(bottom)* Telescope Casual **page 69:** *Photographer: (top)* Michael Thompson; *(bottom)* Telescope Casual **page 70:** *Photographer: (top)* Jessie Walker Associates; *(bottom)* Derek Fell **page 71:** Mark Lohman **page 72:** *Photographer: (top)* Dolores Z. Elliot; *(bottom)* Derek Fell **page 73:** *Photographer: (all)* Telescope Casual **page 74:** *Photographer:* Mark Lohman **page 75:** *Photographer: (all except center right)* John Kelly; *(center right)* Summit Furniture **page 76:** *Photographer:* Mark Lohman **page 79:** *Photographer:* Philip Clayton-Thompson **page 80:** *Photographer: (top)* Broil-master®; *(bottom)* Weber **page 82:** *Photographer:* Mark Lohman **page 83:** *Photographer:* Philip Clayton-Thompson **page 84:** *Photographer:* Tria Giovan **page 86:** *Photographer:* Philip Clayton-Thompson **page 87:** *Photographer:* Philip Clayton-Thompson **page 88:** *Photographer: (top)* Crandall & Crandall; *(bottom)* Michael S. Thompson **page 89:** *Photographer: (top)* Mark Lohman; *(bottom)* Lee Photographers/Ken Graber **page 90:** *Photographer: (top)* Philip Clayton-Thompson; *(bottom left and right)* Jessie Walker **page 91:** *Photographer: (left)* Sub Zero; *(right)* Frontgate **page 92:** *Photographer:* Mark Lohman **page 95:** *Photog-*

rapher: Mark Lohman **page 96:** *Photographer: (top)* Jessie Walker Associates; *(bottom left)* Telescope Casual; *(bottom right)* Mark Lohman **page 97:** *Photographer:* Dolores Z. Elliot **page 98:** *Photographer:* Jessie Walker Associates **page 99:** *Photographer: (top)* Dolores Z. Elliot; *(bottom)* Jessie Walker Associates **page 100:** *Photographer: (top)* Mark Samu; *(bottom)* Dolores Z. Elliot **page 101:** *Photographer:* Tim Street-Porter **page 102:** *Photographer: (top)* H. Armstrong Roberts/ D. Petku; *(bottom)* H. Armstrong Roberts/A. Bolesta **page 103:** *Photographer: (all)* Mark Lohman **page 104:** *Photographer:* California Redwood Association **page 106:** *Photographer:* Michael Thompson **page 107:** *Photographer:* Western Cedar Association **page 108:** *Photographer: (top)* Positive Images; *(bottom)* Derek Fell **page 109:** *Photographer: (top)* Marvin Sloben/California Redwood Association; *(bottom)* Dolphin *Architects:* Walt Schlager **page 110:** California Redwood Association **page 111:** *Photographer: (top)* Crandall & Crandall; *(bottom)* Southern Forest Product Association **page 112:** *Photographer:* Michael Thompson **page 113:** *Photographer:* Western Cedar Association **page 114:** *Photographer: (top)* Trex Decks; *(bottom)* Crandall & Crandall **page 116:** *Photographer:* Summit Furniture **page 117:** *Photographer: (top)* Weber; *(bottom)* ALD Photography **page 118:** Ken Rice/H. Armstrong Roberts **page 122:** *Photographer:* Crandall and Crandall **page 125:** *Photographer:* Brian Vanden Brink **page 126:** *Photographer:* Brain Vanden Brink

Have a home improvement, decorating, or gardening project? Look for these and other fine
Creative Homeowner books at your local home center or bookstore. . .

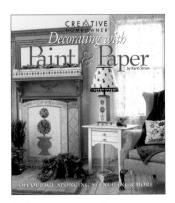

Projects to personalize your rooms with paint and paper. 300 color photos. 176 pp.; 9"x10"
BOOK#: 279723

Learn how to make the most of color. More than 150 color photos. 176 pp.; 9"x10"
BOOK #: 287264

How to create kitchen style like a pro. Over 150 color photographs. 176 pp.; 9"x10"
BOOK #: 279935

How to work with space, color, pattern, texture. Over 300 photos. 256 pp.; 9"x10"
BOOK #: 279667

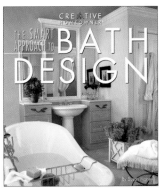

All you need to know about designing a bath. Over 150 color photos. 176 pp.; 9"x10"
BOOK #: 287225

Get the practical information you need to choose window treatments. Over 100 illustrations & 125 photos. 176 pp.; 9"x10"
BOOK #: 279431

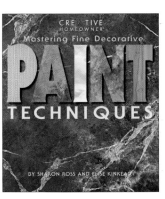

Turn an ordinary room into a masterpiece with decorative faux finishes. Over 40 techniques & 300 photos. 272 pp.; 9"x10"
BOOK #: 279550

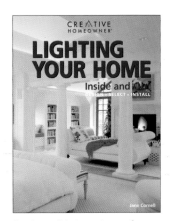

Design a lighting scheme for every room in your home and outdoors. 525 illustrations. 176 pp., 81/2"x107/8"
BOOK#: 277583

Complete houseplant guide. 200 readily available plants; more than 400 photos. 192 pp.; 9"x10"
BOOK #: 275243

Create more beautiful, healthier, lower-maintenance lawns. Over 300 illustrations. 160 pp.; 9"x10"
BOOK #: 274359

How to convert unused space into useful living area. 570 illustrations. 192 pp.; 81/2"x107/8"
BOOK#: 277680

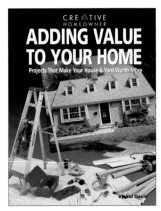

Filled with DIY projects to repair, upgrade, and add value. 500 illustrations. 176 pp.; 81/2"x107/8"
BOOK#: 277006

For more information, and to order direct, call 800-631-7795; in New Jersey 201-934-7100.
Please visit our Web site at www.creativehomeowner.com